Written by Marie-Pierre Klut
Illustrated by Pierre de Hugo

Specialist adviser:
Dr Jane Mainwaring,
The British Museum (Natural History)

ISBN 1 85103 043 3
First published 1988 in the United Kingdom by
Moonlight Publishing Ltd,
36 Stratford Road, London W8

POCKET • WORLDS

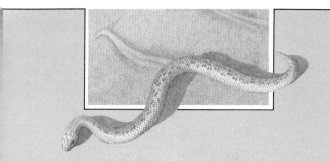

Animal Colours and Patterns

Do you enjoy playing with
dressing-up clothes?

People like dressing-up and disguising themselves – for parties and plays, or just for fun.

In some countries, people disguise themselves in deadly earnest, the better to merge into the forest when they go hunting... This kind of dressing-up to conceal yourself is called **camouflage.**

Animals wear disguises too.

They don't hide for fun, but in order to hunt, or to avoid being hunted. They have skin or shells or fur which match their backgrounds and make them almost impossible to see.

Why are animals different colours?

Animals use colours to tell each other things. The different patterns on birds' wings help them to recognise other birds of the same kind.

Two mandrills can tell that they are both males by the bright blue and red markings on their faces.

It is important for all animals to be able to recognise each other, to tell friends from enemies, and to know their own kind. In most animals the males, who must make themselves attractive to the females, are the brightly coloured ones. They show off until the females choose the one they want to mate with.

When female mandrills are ready to mate, their bottoms turn a brilliant scarlet to attract the males.

Colours are very important for attracting a mate.

The lemur is a monkey-like animal from Madagascar, an island off the coast of Africa. He waves his beautiful black-and-white striped tail in the air, as a signal to his female.

Birds court each other with all sorts of displays: they show off their feathers and cry loudly to each other, beating their wings, swooping and dancing around.

The male and female blue-footed booby, a kind of big sea-bird, court by showing off their blue feet to each other. They look as if they're doing a dance!

The booby is a kind of gannet which lives in colonies on rocky outcrops in the Atlantic.

Frigate-birds, big birds who live along coastlines in northern Europe, make their nests on islands. When it is mating time, the male frigate bird inflates his huge red balloon-like throat to attract any passing females.

Have you ever seen a peacock fanning out his tail in all its finery?

The swaying shape and spectacular, glinting colours charm the peahen.

With their constantly swivelling eyes, chameleons are quick to spot the insects they feed on.

Animals use colour to disguise themselves. Some of them need to hide in order to survive. Some hide from their attackers, others hide to attack.

Watch that chameleon!

Chameleons are a kind of lizard which live in trees in Africa and parts of Asia. They can change colour so quickly they can completely match their backgrounds.

It is almost impossible to see which stem or branch they are sitting on. The colours, or pigments, in their skins, change according to a nervous reaction. If they are frightened, or even if they are just resting, they may change colour. Their background or the time of day affect them too; they may be black or yellow, red or green or white.

Only their ever-moving eyes give chameleons away.

They hardly ever close their eyes as they sit utterly still on a branch, waiting for their prey. Their eyes move independently, so that they can look out in two directions at once! When an insect comes within reach, they snap out their long sticky tongues and catch it.

A sudden noise or movement can make a chameleon change colour too.

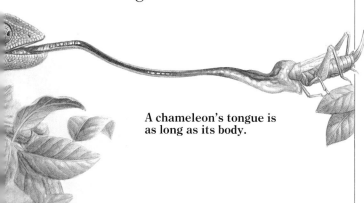

A chameleon's tongue is as long as its body.

Crab-spiders change colour as they move from flower to flower.

Yellow on a yellow flower, as they move to a white flower all their colour gradually fades away, until they are as white as the petals they sit on. Almost invisible, they can easily catch a butterfly or spider and inject it with poison before they eat it.

You need sharp eyes to see an octopus.

It can change colour to match the rocks and sand of its underwater home.

Plaice can match the sand around them. They flick sand over the edges of their bodies to complete the disguise.

 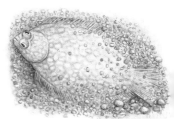

Octopi can make their skin go smooth or bumpy to match the texture of the rocks they're sitting on.

All unknowing, the crabs and lobsters which the octopus likes to eat walk slowly by – until the 'rock' reaches out with its tentacles!

Did you know that the arctic fox (1) changes colour according to the time of year? White as snow in winter, in summer its fur goes darker so that it can hide among the bare rocks.

1

3

2

ike the fox, the ptarmigan (2) and the
rmine (4) change colour from winter to
ummer. The arctic hare (3) and the snowy
wl (5), which live in countries where the
now never melts, are always white.

On the sun-scorched plains of Africa, lionesses flatten themselves on the ground as they watch for their prey; crouching down, they leave no shadow which might give them away.

A baby leopard (1) is protected by his markings, which make him look like a honey-badger (2), one of the fiercest small animals in Africa.

Why does a zebra have stripes?
Zebra stripes disguise the body-shape from hunters – they also put off biting insects which seem dazzled by the stripes. Giraffes have a crazy-paving pattern, leopards have spots. All these patterns are natural camouflage.

gazelle is the same colour as the dry grass of the plains.

In tropical forests, the plants and trees are green all the year round. A lot of the animals and insects that live there are green too.

Others, however, have the most brilliant and brightly-coloured markings. Parrots and parakeets, for instance – their vivid colours make the shape of the birds easy to see. There are few hunters about, so they have no need to hide.

Tigers have stripes which imitate the dark and light of bright sunshine falling through the long, thick grass. They can hide and hunt in safety.

The Malaysian rattlesnake is as green as the plants he hunts and sleeps amongst.

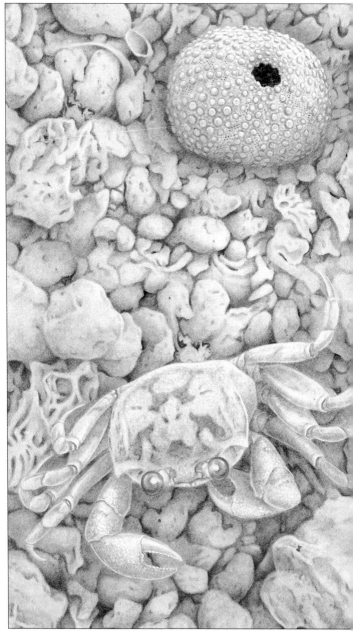

Under the sea, along the coral reefs,
a ghost crab is on the prowl. You can only
see it when it moves. Most of the time it
stays quite still, merging into the
background. Moray eels sway with the
current, half-hidden in a crack in the
rocks, ready to attack.

Some crabs put on a mask! Almost like a
soldier sticking leaves into his helmet, the
porcelain-crab has outgrowths on its shell
that get tangled up with seaweed.
Sometimes the seaweed may even stick to
the crab's shell and help to camouflage it.

The sponge-carrying crab has a live sponge
growing on its shell – the sponge and the
crab grow together. The crab is disguised
by the sponge, and the
sponge feeds off scraps
of food floating up
from the crab's claws.

sponge-carrying crab ▶

Underwater, it's hard to believe your eyes! The stone-fish could not be better named; it looks exactly like a rock on the sea-bed. But spines on its body are tipped with a deadly poison – swimmers in Australia, where it lives, must take care not to tread on it.

A shoal of razor-fish float head-downwards to look like seaweed.

The leaf-fish merges into the background with its transparent tail and stripes all over its body, even across its eyes, to break up its outline.

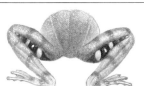

The markings on the back of this tree-frog's legs look like eyes – while an enemy is trying to work out whether it's coming or going, it has had time to run away.

African stinkbugs hang on a twig and make it look as though it has burst into flower.

An almost invisible butterfly

The glasswing butterfly has transparent wings through which you can see the plants and rocks. In America, some forest birds feed on insects by night and keep out of danger during the day by perching, wings down, on a mossy branch – they look almost like pieces of wood themselves. Can you see one in the picture?

The peacock-sphinx butterfly frightens off predators by flashing the huge painted eyes on its wings.

This is a harmless fly. It has borrowed the fierce appearance of the wasp to protect itself.

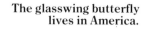

The glasswing butterfly
lives in America.

You think you're picking up a twig,

a leaf or a flower, but it could be an insect!
In some countries, insects disguise
themselves as dry leaves. This is safer than
copying fresh ones. Plants come in so many
different kinds of green that matching one
might make the insect show up against the
others. So the leaf-butterfly matches the
dried leaves and gains safety while it rests.
The Malaysian phyllium looks just like a
small piece of leaf.

The lemon butterfly
takes advantage of its
amazing likeness to a
leaf.

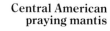

Central American
praying mantis

Greenfly feeding
on a leaf-stem

A feast for ladybirds!
Ladybirds love eating greenfly –
and where there is one there may
soon be hundreds, gathering to feed on
the sweet juices they suck from the plants.

The green praying mantis is well disguised.
It lurks motionless on a stem until it
strikes at insects with its long front legs. It
even eats its own kind if given half a
chance. The female mantis eats the male
even while he is mating with her. The
Central American mantis imitates the
appearance of the climbing
plants it lives near.

European praying mantis

The Sahara Desert is thronged with sand-coloured creatures: fennec foxes (1), jerboas (2) and cheetahs (3) are all the colour of yellow sand. Green plants are rare in the desert – to conceal themselves, animals must be the colour of the land.

The colour of scorpions (4) and lizards (5) alters according to where they live. They are black or grey in rocky regions, yellow and sometimes even white in sandy areas. If a lizard is caught by its tail, the tail will break off and wriggle in the predator's mouth – while the lizard runs away. It soon grows a new tail.

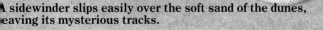

A sidewinder slips easily over the soft sand of the dunes, leaving its mysterious tracks.

If it is attacked, the oyster-catcher,
a conspicuous bird, runs away from its nest,
diverting attention from its well-camouflaged eggs.

Baby animals are weak and easy to attack.

It is very important for them to be able to go unseen. Often the young have different markings from their parents. When the **plover chick** hears its parents' alarm-cries, it flattens itself against the ground until it can hardly be seen. The adult will carefully remove the empty eggshells from the nest – in case their white insides might catch a predator's eye and attract it to where the chicks are sitting.

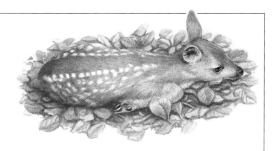

The deer fawn lies crouched in the brown leaves, its head and neck flattened against the ground. Its dappled coat helps it to merge into the shifting light and shadows of the forest. As the fawn grows older, its coat will darken.

The nightjar and its chicks merge so perfectly into their leafy background that they can hardly be seen at all.
To make its camouflage even more perfect, the mother bird closes her enormous eyes, and watches the world through the narrowest of slits.

Play hide-and-seek with the animals.
Can you find them as they hide in the different landscapes in these pictures?

Arctic hare – Ermine – Ptarmigan

Frog – Lemon butterfly – Praying mantis

When you go animal-watching, you will see more if you wear a leaf-coloured disguise and stay as still as you can.

Scorpion – African gazelle – Lizard

Razor-fish – Ghost crab – Stone-fish

Pocket Worlds – building up into a child's first encyclopaedia: